Nurturing A Gentle Heart

Exploring spirituality
with pre-schoolers

**Kristen
Hobby**

ISBN: 1-4392-0558-2
ISBN-13: 9781439205587

Visit www.booksurge.com to order additional copies.

Book dedication:
To Andrew and Isabella

Acknowledgements and Thanks

I would firstly like to thank Kylie Lloyd who suggested I write this book. I would also like to thank the students and parents at the Early Learning Centre at St. Leonards College, Cornish campus Victoria for their support and encouragement, and especially the teaching staff; Kirsty Liljegren, Cathy Phillips, Rebecca Wooderson and Kate Campbell. The following people have read my manuscript and provided valuable feedback; Philippa Caris, Georgia Gregg and my father Kevin Mark. To my parents in law Faye and David Hobby for their feedback on cover design.

To my secret writing group (you know who you are, T, AC & A). It is a privilege to know such a wonderful group of talented, uncompromising and intelligent women. My life is richer for knowing you all.

To the Lakeside writing group, thank you for all your valuable feedback and encouragement.

Thank you to Jennie Savage and Marcia Richards for your prayerful support.

To the wonderful team at Booksurge, Lynn, Helen, Sarah and the team, you have made this project a joy to complete.

To Chris James who bought the first copy before it was even finished.

To my beautiful daughter Isabella who created the artwork and is the reason this book was created. You constantly amaze and delight me. And finally to my wonderful husband Andrew whose encouragement and support know no bounds.

The publication of this book signals to the community that we ought to slow down and listen to our children. Carlina Rinaldi, pedagogical Director from Reggio Children talks about today's society; fast cars, fast food, and with that comes fast children. The effects of this are starting to surface as we are witness to many children being diagnosed with various stress related disorders and learning difficulties.

Could the desire to provide our children with the best opportunities by involving them in many activities be having the opposite effect to what we intend? When do we allow children the time to stop and to be; time to not know what to do, to invent a game or look around them and be resourceful. Are we so busy protecting children that we eliminate the opportunity for them to grow from taking risks and making mistakes?

As an early years educator, I am privileged to be working in a way where children can stop to ponder, to investigate, to wonder and to imagine. When we are really open to how children are viewing the world, it opens up so many possibilities and we ourselves are open the wonder and mystery of life. Children are natural enquirers, fascinated and engaged with the world around them, it is our role as adults to support them with this natural connection. Learning is so powerful when it is meaningful, unhurried and supported by the companionship of another, a child or an adult. Our natural environment provides a wealth of opportunities for discovery and awe inspiring moments of learning. My own happiest memories from childhood are from occasions spent outdoors, interacting with nature and , where time seemed limitless.

Kristen Hobby invites us through this book to be that companion with children, to support them in their fascination with the world around them.

Kirsty Liljegren is the Director of the Early Learning Centre at St. Leonard's College Cornish Campus and on the Executive Committee of the Reggio Emilia Australia Information Exchange.

Contents

Children Learn What They Live

If a child lives with criticism
They learn to condemn.
If a child lives with hostility
They learn to fight
If a child lives with ridicule
They learn to be shy.
If a child lives with shame
They learn to be guilty.
If a child lives with tolerance
They learn to be patient.
If a child lives with encouragement
They learn confidence.
If a child lives with praise
They learn to appreciate.
If a child lives with fairness
They learn justice.
If a child lives with security
They learn to have faith.
If a child lives with approval

They learn to like themselves.
If a child lives with acceptance and friendship
They learn to give love in the world.

Dorothy Law Nolte

Introduction

We all want our children to grow up to be happy and healthy. We wish them to find fulfilment and be resilient in the tough times. Are children ever too young to begin to learn to trust their inner wisdom? At what age do they even develop an inner wisdom? Can very young children have a sense of their spirit? What can we do as parents, teachers and carers of children during their early years to help this happen?

As a parent of a four-year-old I often wonder about these questions. Am I expecting too much from my daughter or am I encouraging her to grow and develop in a holistic way? How do I as a mother tend to her health and wellbeing at all stages of her childhood? I hope this book will answer these questions for you and provide you with some resources to help you and your children.

In today's busy world, I would like to offer an alternative to the two-minute grab for attention that is our lives. We are inundated with information every minute of every day by TV, newspapers, billboards and the Internet. Sometimes it can be refreshing to just 'be' for a while, to turn off the outside and listen to our own messages. I wish to offer the alternative path, a place of quiet away from the everyday, a place where we can feel safe, happy and at peace.

How to Use this Book

The book is arranged in chapters following the theme of the heart. You will find the following chapters:

- The Gentle Heart
- The Peaceful heart
- The Present and Aware Heart
- The Creative Heart
- The Natural Heart
- The Reflective Heart

Each chapter invites you to look at your child in a new way. I have included activities and simple meditations or relaxation exercises in each chapter for you to try. Feel free to dip into whichever chapter is useful at the time; you don't need to read the chapters sequentially. You may find a particular mediation or activity that your child or prefers; if that is the case, use it as often as you need. If you sense that your child is anxious or upset, a few minutes of just quietly focusing on breathing may help, or an imaginary journey along a beautiful beach can calm him or her.

My aim in writing this book is to provide parents, carers and teachers with resources to gently invite young children to experience relaxation and quiet, to learn to be happy within themselves and to come to know that there is deep wisdom within each of us. If children are introduced to concepts such as loving themselves and others, being aware of their own feelings, and being comfortable with silence at an early age, this will lead to greater resilience and inner strength. By getting to know themselves and trusting their feelings, children will begin to find their own gifts that they can share with the world.

The underlying principles of this book are to nurture awareness of ourselves and our feelings, to learn to be honest and loving toward ourselves and to grow in awareness that we are special, unique and loved. I have kept the meditations simple and used topics such as love, wisdom and kindness. I would like to invite your children to know wisdom and love for themselves and others.

Chapter 1
Nurturing a Gentle Heart

**What Is Spirituality and
How Does It Apply to Preschoolers?**

The focus of this book is around children's *spirituality*. It might be helpful to define what we mean by spirituality.

'Spirituality is about our sense of connection with the sacred.'

– *David Tacey (1998)*

Spirituality simply means our connection to the spirit, that part within us that connects us to each other and the source of all life. I want this book to be an inclusive one and not to exclude anyone of the basis of faith or religion. Some may easily use the title God as the source of life, but I encourage you use to use whatever word, term or feeling makes you and your children feel most comfortable. You might like *love*, *life* or *divine higher being*. It really doesn't matter because the focus of this book is to help children begin to recognise their own inner wisdom and their own sense of uniqueness and giftedness.

When my daughter began kindergarten at three years old, I was invited by her teacher to offer meditation to the children. I began by running some guided imagery meditations with a journey along a beach. I started with deep breathing then engaged the five senses, encouraging the children to imagine sitting down, their bare feet caressing the sand while the waves came in and out. I concluded with returning to breathing before I asked them what they had seen.

I was amazed by their responses. They saw purple starfish, sharks in the water, crabs walking along the beach and birds flying above them. I asked what colour the crabs were and they went on to describe them vividly—colours, shapes and sizes. When I asked the children how it felt being on the beach, many were able to respond. Some said, 'good,' 'relaxed' or 'warm.'

After a few weeks of doing this, even the most active child began to relax and become quiet. Parents thanked me, saying how much their children had enjoyed the meditation. One mother told me how her daughter had set her dolls up in a circle and told them to close their eyes, as they were going to do some meditation. Another child told his mum that he now knew what to do if he got upset: 'I just breathe deeply.' I took my daughter for a walk to the local park; when we walked past a bench, she said to me, 'Let's sit here and do some meditation, Mummy. Now come on, close your eyes, breathing in, breathing out.'

Later I tried a simple relaxation meditation with the children in which I imagined a warm golden light starting at the top of their heads and travelling slowly down their bodies. The children responded beautifully, so I even introduced a one-minute silence during which I left them bathed in the light. When I asked them to tell me what it was like, a number of them said they felt warm or even hot. One girl said that she saw a starfish, but she may have associated my voice with a trip to the beach!

I was so encouraged by this exercise that I wanted to write a book, hoping to introduce other parents and carers to meditation and relaxation that they could use with their children. I have taken adult relaxation techniques and modified them for young children. In many cases I have written my own meditations, which is not hard to do, using the guidelines of beginning and ending with breathing and then undertaking a simple journey to a forest, a garden or any special place. You will find notes at the end to help you write your own meditations. Perhaps you have a holiday house or another special spot you visit often where your child feels safe and relaxed. If your child loves animals, invent a scene in which the animals visit the child in a way that is safe. Above all, always create environments where your child feels safe and secure and that no harm can come to him or her.

These meditations also work well as an exercise before bed. If you find it helps settle your child down to sleep, then use it in that way. There is no right or wrong way to use this book. Make it your own; use it when you feel it is right.

Discernment

Discernment is the process of getting to know ourselves and beginning to identify what is helpful, life-giving and energizing in our lives. It is also coming to know what is unhelpful, harmful or even destructive to us. We all have the wisdom within to know what is good for us and what is unhelpful. Our feelings as well as our bodies give us clues. At times we all have had a hunch about someone, or we may have had a physical reaction to an event. We might feel a tightening in the chest, shoulders or right deep down in the gut.

But sometimes unlocking this wisdom can be difficult or elusive. If we can begin to unlock this knowledge, we become more in tune with ourselves, more able to handle life's knocks and more able to help others around us. Initially children may not have the vocabulary to articulate feelings but over time and with practice they can develop this gift. It is a gift we give ourselves, the freedom to love ourselves as we are and to be happy being ourselves.

As parents we want our children to be loving and to be loved. If we could wish for anything for them, certainly high on the list would be a deep desire that they always be surrounded with people who love and respect them and celebrate the unique gifts they bring to our world.

When I refer to a 'gentle heart,' I am referring to a way of being that is kind and loving, not harsh or stern; a way of looking at the world and the people around us as kind. This also extends to being gentle on ourselves. We are always our own worst critics. But what would our lives be like if we grew to love ourselves, to celebrate the happy times and to choose to learn from the unhappy or difficult moments rather than berating ourselves? If we make mistakes, we must recognise that we tried and that the outcome was not what we had hoped—but that is okay. Of course we want our children to feel challenged to always do their best, but what real value comes from berating ourselves endlessly for an unwanted outcome? Mistakes are often the only way to learn.

We nurture a gentle heart by learning to be kind to ourselves. Children of gentle heart will be accepting of other people and respectful of other people's views even when they might not agree with them. As parents we can help by acknowledging the effort—'I can see you really tried to get this right'—and acknowledging when things don't go as they had hoped—'I can see you tried hard, and it can be disappointing when things don't work out the way we would like' or 'That was a good effort, let's try again.'

Building resilience in children begins by experiencing and reflecting on both the joyous moments and the difficult ones. If we are able to see difficult events as learning experiences rather than things we need to avoid, we can build a healthy view of ourselves. In this way, you are acknowledging the disappointment and valuing your child's experience. You are empathizing with him or her by admitting that things don't always go the way we would like. This can lead to greater resilience and strength.

We can model gentleness as parents by explaining simple examples like burning a piece of toast—'Oops, I let the toast burn, I will have to keep an eye on it next time.' This may sound glib, but it allows our children a glimpse of our inner thoughts and feelings and how we cope with life's events.

Saying Sorry

I think one of the most helpful ways of modelling a gentle heart is to be able to apologise to children. Sometimes, despite our best efforts, we get things wrong; we forget to buy the milk or we accidently bump them when we are dressing them. From the earliest ages it is invaluable to be able say to our children, 'I'm sorry, I didn't mean to do that.' Even when we don't think they understand, it sets up a respectful relationship.

Our Image of God and the Divine

Often in my work as a Spiritual Director, I listen to people as they talk about their sense of God. What often arises is an image of God as judge in the sky, one who is quick to punish or sees all and is just waiting for us to make a mistake. When we explore this image we may find that it originates in our childhood, perhaps as is an experience of Sunday school or from something we heard our own parents say. This image often stops people from becoming all that they can be. They live their lives trying to be 'good' or 'righteous,' afraid of making mistakes and being judged.

As I reflect upon this I wonder what might happen if we were able to embrace a loving God who loves us unconditionally and is always there supporting and affirming us? What if this was our first understanding of God, allowing us to live our lives free from a judging God? For us to create this understanding for our children, we must first embrace it and know it for ourselves.

Reflection for Parents

What is your earliest memory of God?

What is your current image of God?

How would you like to understand God?

What might your life be like if you were to embrace an unconditionally loving God?

This is not a simple exercise; it may take many weeks or months to be able to move to a more loving image of God.

Explaining God to Children

You may choose not to try to explain God to your child, and that is fine. If you would like to, however, you may find these guidelines helpful.

- Children have an amazing ability to grasp the concept of an all-loving God.
- Consider explaining the image of God as Creator who made all the trees and animals and ourselves.
- Invite children to see God as friend and confidant, someone who loves them for being just themselves, not because of anything they do but because of who they are.
- Use the image of God being within us, that we each have a part of God inside us that is always there to help and guide us. If we listen to this part we will always know the best way forward.

- Try not to use any terms that are fear-based such as, 'God can tell when you are naughty' or 'God will punish you.' At a young age these images can frighten children and even stifle their creativity.

Using Meditation with Young Children

I have used two types of meditations in this book: guided meditation and relaxation mediations.

Guided meditation is an exercise in imagination. It gently leads children to a new environment such as a beach or a forest or even a loving place (such as loving embrace meditation below). Starting with a breathing exercise helps to settle children down and help them focus. This mediation engages all five senses.

Recent research has shown just how important imagination is for the brain. For the brain, there is very little difference between going for a walk on the beach and simply imagining you are there. It is also why imagining the outcome you would like or achieving a goal can be so powerful. You are telling yourself that it is possible.

These meditations end with a breathing exercise. Try to read through each meditation very slowly, pausing slightly at the end of each line. You can do these meditations either sitting up or lying down, inside or outside.

It is useful to reflect on the experience with your child at the end of each meditation. I find it helpful to reflect using the five senses (see below). It is also good idea to invite children to reflect on how they felt or what feelings arose during the meditation. This is something that is easier to do as children get older, but it is good to begin to ask them at any age; they will become more able to express their feelings with practice. Children may also like to draw a picture of the experience, so have some pencils or crayons handy.

I like to include a few minutes of silent toward the end of the meditation. To begin with this is quite difficult for children, but if you do it regularly you can slowly increase the time. To begin with I might start with twenty to thirty seconds and gradually build it up to a few minutes.

You will probably find also that children won't keep their eyes closed for very long—that is fine. You might find it useful to use a candle and encourage them to look at this when they open their eyes.

Relaxation meditation focuses more on breathing and relaxing parts of the body. I have included both types in this book for you to try. You may like to use the same one or mix it up until you find one that your child prefers. You can still reflect after these types of meditations by asking questions about each sense and inviting the child to draw the experience.

How Often?

There is no right or wrong here. If your child responds well it would be great to do it every day, say before a nap or bedtime; or you may find once a week or so is fine. You might use it when your child seems a little wound up or anxious. You can also explain about focusing on breathing to help if he or she is angry or upset.

Meditations that Can Help

Loving Kindness Meditation

To create an outward feeling of love is to recognise that all living beings are precious. The loving kindness meditation is a way to cultivate the mind of love by wishing ourselves and others well. We start by developing feelings of loving-kindness for ourselves. We then do the same for someone we love.

To start, close your eyes, relax and begin by focusing on your breathing.
Breathing in
Breathing out
Breathing in
Breathing out
Breathing in
Breathing out
Breathing in
Breathing out

The first step is to surround yourself with love.
Picture yourself surrounded by loving-kindness.
You are loved.
You are unique.

The next step is to send loving-kindness to someone you love. Think about your mum and dad, brothers and sisters, grandparents, aunts, uncles, cousins, friends.

You may like to choose one very special person.
Silence for some time—maybe thirty to sixty seconds
Now surround each person you love with your
love and kindness.
Silence for some time—maybe thirty to sixty seconds
When you are ready open your eyes.

Body Relaxation Meditation

Lie down, find a comfortable position and close your eyes.
Breathing in
Breathing out
Breathing in
Breathing out
Breathing in
Breathing out
Breathing in
Breathing out

Now imagine a warm light coming and shining on you. This light begins on the top of your head. The light now moves down on to your face. Feel the warm light on your face. The light now moves down on to your neck. Feel the warm light on your neck. The light now moves down on to your shoulders. Feel the warm light on your shoulders. The light now moves down on to the tops of your arms. Feel the warm light on the tops of your arms. The light now moves down on to your forearms. Feel the warm light on your forearms. The light now moves down on to your hands. Feel the warm light on your hands. The light now moves down on to each finger and your thumbs. Feel the warm light on each finger and your thumbs. Now the light moves to your chest. Feel the warm light on your chest. The light now moves down on to your tummy. Feel the warm light on your tummy. The light now moves down on to the tops of your legs. Feel the warm light on the tops of your legs. The light now moves down to your knees. Feel the warm light on your knees. The light now moves down on to your feet. Feel the warm light on your feet. The light now moves on to each of your toes. Feel the warm light on each toe. The light is now over your whole body. Feel the warm light on your whole body.

(a few moments of silence)

When you are ready, gently open your eyes and sit up.

Summary

- Spirituality simply means our connection to the spirit, that part within us that connects us to each other and the source of all life.
- Discernment is the process of getting to know ourselves and beginning to identify what is helpful, life-giving and energizing in our lives. It is recognizing the wisdom we all have within us.
- We nurture a gentle heart by learning to be kind to ourselves. A child of gentle heart is accepting and respectful of other people.
- Saying sorry to our children is really important, even when they may seem too young to understand it. It sets up a model of respect.
- Guided meditations focus on a journey; it may be a walk along a beach, a stroll through a forest or flower-laden garden
- Relaxation meditations centre around relaxing both our minds and bodies.

Chapter 2
The Peaceful Heart

This chapter will guide you through some activities and meditations to develop a more peaceful and calm outlook for your child's life. When we practice times of quiet without the outside noise of TVs, radios and other sounds, we can come to know ourselves and tap into the wisdom that we all possess. Everyone, even young children, can begin to learn what is important to them, what they enjoy and what they do not.

When we learn to be still for even short periods of time, we begin to know and befriend our feelings. Feelings are not to be scared of or avoided; in fact, they tell us so much about ourselves that they are wonderful indicators of what is really going on in us. As adults, we know when we are in situations that make us feel uncomfortable; we recognise when we are doing something we love and feel grateful for, and we also know when we are doing things that don't quite feel right.

Children can learn at a very young age about recognising feelings and honouring them. We can practice this with them. They may be obviously frustrated by trying to do an activity, for example, open a jar. They may even throw the item away. A useful response might be 'I can see that you are angry, but let's have another go at it' or 'I can see that this is upsetting you, but maybe we could try opening it together.' This way, you are not attacking the child as a person, nor are you attacking the child's actions; instead, you are acknowledging how the child is feeling and giving permission for those feelings to exist.

You can begin at a very young age, two or three, to ask children how they are feeling. In the beginning, they may not be able to respond; but as you practice this, children will begin to respond with feelings such as *good*, *tired* or *sad*. I have noticed that young children will sometimes use the word *sad* for a range of other emotions, so it can be helpful to ask them more about this word. Questions such as 'Tell me what is making you sad' or 'Tell me about this sad feeling' can be useful to help children explore the feeling a little more. You may find sadness is sometimes more about frustration or anger.

It is important to stress to children that feelings aren't good or bad although it often feels nicer to have feelings such as happiness or joy rather than anger or sadness. Children should know that all feelings are valid and that all feelings tell us something about ourselves. There are five basic emotions: grief, anger, envy, fear and love. By allowing our children to freely express these emotions in a way that is safe, they will grow up having a healthy view of these emotions.

Grief is a normal emotion for all of us in that it tells us that we have lost something that was valuable to us. For children this can mean a loved one, a pet or a favourite toy. Grief is a normal response to loss. If children are told that their grief is not important, that it was only a silly toy, this can lead them to feel disrespected. Grief that isn't allowed to be expressed can be suppressed and may turn into depression at a later stage. As parents, we need to create an environment in which grief is accepted and honoured. When this is done, children will grow up being able to express grief and move through it quickly.

Anger is a useful emotion as well; it tells us when our boundaries have been violated or that feelings have not been respected. If children are told not to be angry then they grow up thinking anger is wrong and will try and suppress it. Anger can then turn into rage, which is a very unhelpful emotion. When anger is allowed to be expressed by children, they grow up knowing it is okay to be angry and will move through anger quickly.

Envy is a very normal part of childhood. All children will look at other children, cousins, siblings and friends, and want what they want. A toy that lies untouched until one child picks it up is suddenly the toy everyone wants to play with. The message we often portray is that envy is wrong. As parents and carers, it is vital that we honour these feelings of envy so children learn to work through the emotion. Envy that isn't expressed can turn into jealousy.

Fear is such a normal emotion for all of us. We fear what we don't understand, we fear death and we fear rejection by others. We spend a lot of time fearing the unknown. Fear can be a helpful emotion when it teaches us to be cautious, to tread carefully. But allowing fear to dominate our lives can stop us from really experiencing life. Children, however, do need to be able to express fear and have that emotion respected. Minimising fear by saying 'There is nothing to be scared of' or 'You are acting like a baby' only causes children to suppress their fear. Suppressed fear can turn to panic.

Finally, there is love. When children are offered love freely and without conditions, they learn to express love themselves. When love is controlled and manipulated, children learn that their natural love is wrong. The greatest gift we can give our children is unconditional love. This may sound simple and obvious, yet to be able offer unconditional love we need to love ourselves. When we haven't been offered unconditional love ourselves, we may grow up thinking we are unlovable.

Reflection for the Parents

The path to peace begins with self-awareness. The more we befriend ourselves and notice our thoughts and feelings, the more we can reconcile all the parts of ourselves. One way to begin this process is through your own meditation. This can be as simple as setting aside five to ten minutes each day. Begin with some gentle breathing and just become aware of the thoughts that come to you; don't try to change them, just let them drift by. You can do this all through the day; just become aware of your thoughts.

- What do you notice?
- Do you have the same thoughts recurring over and over?
- Are your thoughts mostly negative or positive?

If you do find your thoughts mostly negative you can begin to change this. Each time a negative thought enters your head, such as 'I'm never going to get it right' or 'I always mess up,' notice how words such as *never* and *always* leave you nowhere to go and leave you feeling flat and uninspired. You can reframe these statements to something that is a little gentler on yourself, such as 'I really find this task difficult.' It acknowledges the difficultly but doesn't allow you to condemn your whole self.

By increasing awareness of our thoughts, we can then begin to identify them in our children. When our children say things such as 'I always fall over,' you can gently guide them by saying, 'I am a good runner but I sometimes fall over when I am not watching where I am going.' This will help your child's confidence and sense of self.

Reflections for Children

A really useful exercise for small children is to ask them at the end of the day, at dinnertime, or at bedtime to think about the day they have had. You may like to ask them:

- What was the best thing about today?
- What did you enjoy the most?
- What made you laugh today?
- What was the happiest thing you did today?

You may also want to contrast this with questions such as:

- What did you enjoy the least today?
- What was the worst thing about today?
- Did anything upset you today?

For young children, this can be a challenging exercise because their sense of time is quite different to ours; events that occurred weeks or months ago can seem like today or yesterday. But it doesn't really matter what event the child chooses; this is an exercise in discernment that, if done regularly, will begin to create a space where children feel comfortable reflecting on their day and begin to notice what they really enjoyed or didn't enjoy. There will always be things that we don't like doing, like cleaning or packing up or going shopping with a parent, and it is important to explore these, too.

These questions can be a wonderful starting point to a conversation. For example, a child may say, 'I really liked playing with Sam today.' You can then ask why he or she enjoys playing with Sam or what they did together. You will often be surprised with what young children will discern as the best part of the day. It may be something simple like watching some ants or looking at clouds.

This exercise can be continued right through to your life. I often use the time when I am in bed getting ready to go to sleep to reflect back on my day and think about what I found the most enjoyable or life-giving and also what I found the hardest or most challenging. This exercise, when performed regularly, will help you to see what in your life is the most energizing, as well as places you are placing your energies that are actually draining you.

One of the aims of the book is to introduce the idea of quiet for young children—to introduce the concept of simply *being* rather than *doing*. This may appear to be a little esoteric for young children, but it is a valuable gift we can give them. We live in a society of doing-ness; we are bombarded with messages of activities, playing games, going to adventure parks, playing sports and renovating the house. There is nothing wrong with these things. They all make up the richness that is life. However, if children only receive the message that they need to be doing things all the time—and worse, that they are only valued as people if they are doing things—then that can be an unhelpful message.

So how do we impart to our children the message that it is okay just to be? The most effective way is to model this ourselves. Spend time just talking or being outside enjoying the outdoors. Model to your children that it is okay to sit down with a cup of tea in a sunny spot or to chat with friends and family. You may choose to sit around the dinner table after the meal just talking about the day. It doesn't have to be for long periods of time, but this modelling is invaluable. Sometimes on a walk or when you are out shopping, you may have opportunities to simply sit on a bench and watch people go by.

Silence is a wonderful place for imagination. For example, when you are stopping or people watching you might like to ask your child questions like these:

- I wonder how old that tree is?
- I wonder what is in those shopping bags?
- What type of house might that person live in?

The responses don't matter, but it can be fun to imagine that there are crocodiles in the shopping bags and that this man lives in a tree house. We are not in any way judging people. The exercise is just one of imagination.

Quiet Time

You might like to introduce the idea of quiet time to your children. This is particularly useful for children who have stopped having an afternoon nap but still struggle to get through till bedtime. Talk with your child about the idea of finding quiet things to do and ask him or her for feedback on what might be quiet activities. You might like to start with a shorter time period and build it up to a longer one. Some activities you might like to try are these:

- Listening to gentle music
- Looking at picture books
- Setting up a rug outside with some books or colouring
- Playing a meditation CD
- Setting up some puzzles
- Playing with building blocks

Listening to Our Children

When we think about people we know who are good listeners, what descriptions come to mind? What do they do to show they are really listening? What is their body language like? If you can remember an occasion when you felt really listened to, how did you feel?

Now think about a situation in which you weren't listened to. Perhaps you were trying to get your point across and didn't feel the other person gave you the opportunity. Perhaps the other person didn't acknowledge what you were saying. How did that make you feel?

When we think about really being listened to, feelings that might arise include feeling understood, feeling valued and feeling like our opinions mattered. When we think about not being listened to, words that come to mind are *ignored*, *unimportant* and *brushed aside*. These are really powerful emotions.

We can all improve how well we listen. As we reflect upon the day, we may see examples in which we didn't listen well to our children or our partner or the other people in our lives. To be a good listener, we need to really want to listen, to want to understand the other's viewpoint.

Here are some more tips for conversations with children as well as adults:

- Try asking as many open ended questions as you can. Open questions begin with *how, what, when, why* and *who*. Questions may also start with statements, such as 'Tell me more about that.'
- Avoid closed questions that only require a yes, no or one-word answer such as 'Did you have fun today?'
- Listen with your whole body. Where possible try and get down to your child's level.
- Maintain good eye contact.
- Try to put aside your own thoughts, judgments and ideas and instead really hear what the other person is saying.
- Set up a quiet space to have a conversation away from as many distractions as possible.
- Let your child know that you are interested in his or her ideas.
- Communicate to him or her your own sense of curiosity and wonder.
- You might like to reflect back to your child what he or she said in order to communicate that you are listening; for example, 'So you really found the puzzle difficult.'
- If you don't understand something, ask your child to repeat it or try another way of explaining it.

- Enjoy the conversation, laugh with your child and if appropriate share some of your thoughts and ideas about the topic.
- Try not to jump in and finish your child's sentences and thoughts but allow him or her the space to come to conclusions
- Give your child plenty of time and space. Practice this regularly.
- Thank your child for sharing with you.

What Does Peace Mean?

Peace is a really interesting concept. People wish for world peace or even a peaceful Christmas, but what do we mean by this? Do we mean everyone is nice and gets on perfectly and there is never a bad word? I think peace is more realistic than that. A peacemaker is someone who recognises that as long as there are people living in relationship with one another, there will be conflict and difficulties; but that there are always peaceful ways to resolve that conflict.

Resolving conflict need not require force, abuse or violence; there are ways of resolving conflict that are respectful, caring and peaceful. To be peacemakers and people who work towards creating peace is not an easy thing. It requires courage and commitment to just live and create mutual understanding between all people.

We can continue to talk about peace abstractly, but the challenge is to actively respond to the values that support and maintain violence as the norm. I believe that violence is not a given. It is a choice. And we all have the opportunity to learn to choose differently. I believe that to do this effectively there needs to be leadership and modelling of peaceful resolutions of conflict. This can be very difficult when there are many countries in the world currently at war with one another.

I believe that as parents and carers, we can show another way of being. To bring about a culture of peace, where differences are respected and where human beings treat each other with compassion, is both a simple and a profound goal.

Human beings are capable of such amazing acts of compassion, yet we are also capable of such violence and debasement of other humans. The challenge is now before us to evolve just as rapidly as generous, tolerant and peaceful beings who work together for the common good.

It was John Dewey who said,

> *The only way to abolish war is to make peace heroic.*

It is helpful to remember that children all learn in different ways: some respond creatively, for example through drawing or painting; some learn best through stories; and others may need to experience the difference between peaceful and non-peaceful means.

The next story is about peace in the world. You might like to share it with your children.

Sunflowers for Peace

The Message of the Sunflowers: A Magic Symbol of Peace By Georgianna Moore

Once upon a time the earth was even more beautiful than it is today. The water was pure and deep, reflecting within itself the sunlight that gave life to all the creatures beneath the waves.

The earth was green with many kinds of trees and plants. These provided food and shelter to the birds, the animals and to all people. At night the air was so clear that the starlight gave a glow almost as bright as the moon.

The people of the earth lived close to nature. They understood it and honoured it and never took more than what they needed from it. The people lived in peace, so they prospered and began to build many nations all around the world according to nature's climate.

But one day, a terrible thing happened. A strange spirit of greed entered the hearts of the people. They began to be jealous of one another and were no longer satisfied with all the good things they already had. The nations wanted more and more of everything: more land, more water, more resources. They squeezed precious minerals from the earth to build terrible weapons to defend their nations from other greedier nations. They killed one another. They polluted the air and the water with poisons. Nature began to die. This is called war. War is ugly. It destroys love and hope and peace.

Then one day a magical thing occurred. The birds of the air, the animals of the land and the creatures beneath the waters came to an agreement: if they were to survive, something would have to be done to stop these wars. Only through peace could their world survive.

'We cannot speak the human language,' they declared, 'and people can no longer understand ours. We must find among us a symbol of peace so brilliant that all who see it will stop and remember that peace and sharing are beautiful.'

'I am what you need,' said a golden sunflower. 'I am tall and bright. My leaves are food for the animals, my yellow petals can turn plain cloth to gold, my seeds are many and are used for food by all living beings. Yet the seeds I drop upon the ground can take root and I will grow again and again. I can be your symbol of peace.'

All nature rejoiced, and it was decided that the birds would each take one sunflower seed and fly over every nation to plant the seed in the earth as a gift. The seeds took root and grew, and the sunflowers multiplied. Wherever the sunflowers grew, there seemed to be a special golden glow in the air. The people could not ignore such a magical sight.

Soon they began to understand the message of the sunflowers, so they decided to destroy all of their terrible weapons and to put an end to the greed and to the fear of war. They chose the sunflower as a symbol of peace and new life for all the world to recognise and understand.

A ceremony was celebrated by planting a whole field of sunflowers. Artists painted pictures of the sunflowers, writers wrote about them and the people of the world were asked to plant more sunflower seeds as a symbol of remembrance.

All nature rejoiced once more as the golden sunflowers stood tall with their faces turned eastward to the rising sun, then following the sun until its setting in the west. They gave their goodness to the world so that everyone who sees a sunflower will know that the golden light of peace is beautiful.

Reflections for Parents

- In what ways does this story touch you?
- What might it be like to live a peaceful life?
- How can you model peace in your life?

Reflections for Children

You might like to talk about this story with your child. Here are some helpful questions to begin:

- What do you think we mean by greed?
- What do you think we mean by peace?

You might like to plant your own sunflowers. As they grow, you can talk to you children about the way peace starts small, like a sunflower seed, and grows to something large and beautiful that everyone can see. When the flowers open, you and your children might like to think about ways in your life you can turn to face the sun every day, living a life of peace.

Respecting Children's Choices

One of the most helpful ways of modelling respectful and gentle behaviour is to offer choices to young children. 'Would you like a drink of water or milk?' When they are not co-operating choices can also be effective. 'If you help pack up your toys we can start painting.' When they start to pack up, praise their efforts, affirming that they made a good choice. When they misbehave, use this as an opportunity to reflect on their choice. Ask them if they are making good choices or bad choices.

We were trying very hard to have our daughter Isabella give up her dummy at night. When a film came to the cinemas, we thought she would like it if we offered her the choice. 'You can see the movie if you give up your dummy for one night.' She gave it a lot of thought and then announced that no, she'd rather not see the film and keep her dummy. On to Plan B!

Choices can be empowering tools that allow children a sense of control over their behaviour. This doesn't require force but is a peaceful means of settling disputes.

Some Meditations to Try

Loving Embrace

Find a comfortable position.
Close your eyes.
Big breath in, breathing all the way down to your toes.
Breathing out
Breathing in
Breathing out
Breathing in
Breathing out
Breathing in
Breathing out

Imagine you are entering a large house. The house is beautifully decorated with lovely pictures and statues. Ahead of you is a doorway. Through the doorway is a room. As you enter the room you find it is filled with all the people who love you. You see your parents and grandparents, brothers and sisters, friends and pets. Take a few moments to look at each person; move around the room and feel their loving care and affection for you. They are all there for you. They all love you and only want to be happy and safe.

(a few moments of silence)

When you are ready open your eyes and come back to the room.

The Garden

Find a comfortable position.
Close your eyes. Big breath in, breathing all the way down to your toes.
Breathing out
Breathing in
Breathing out
Breathing in
Breathing out
Breathing in
Breathing out

Imagine you are in a beautiful garden. All around you are plants and flowers. There are birds flying in the sky and animals like monkeys and possums or squirrels in the trees. It is perfectly safe; nothing can hurt you in this garden. You might like to smell a flower. You see a tall tree, feel its bark. There are some safe berries to eat; what do they taste like? What else do you see? What do you hear?

(a few moments of silence)

When you are ready open your eyes and come back to the room.

Summary

- Feelings are an integral part of ourselves. They show us what is really happening for us. They are neither good nor bad. From a very young age, children are able to express their feelings.
- There are five main emotions from which all other emotions spring: grief, anger, envy, fear and love.
- A peacemaker is someone who recognises that as long as there are people living in relationship with one another, there will be conflict and difficulties; but that there are always peaceful ways to resolve that conflict.
- An effective strategy for parents is to offer choices to our children. Praise good choices and reflect together on bad choices.

Chapter 3
The Present and Aware Heart

Children have an amazing capacity for noticing what is happening and perhaps what has changed. 'You are wearing a different top, Mum' or 'The old house has gone from the corner.' They notice things that as adults we seem to be completely unaware of. I'm sure that we once had the same ability to notice things, and that as we have gotten older we have lost this ability. To live fully in the moment is a gift that we can encourage in both our children and ourselves—to not be thinking constantly of what has happened to us in the past or worrying about what is to come (remember, ninety percent of what we worry about never eventuates) but to live fully in the moment.

Try this for a task you are about to perform; it doesn't matter if it is a mundane or everyday task (these actually work the best, which is why monks often choose the most arduous or boring tasks as meditation). It may be folding up the washing or making a cup of tea. Engage every sense, hear the sound of the kettle boiling and whistling, hear the water being poured into the cup, smell the aroma of the tea or coffee, watch how the water swirls and changes colour, taste the sugar and milk before you add them to the cup, feel the warmth and texture of the cup in your hands, feel the taste of the liquid upon your tongue and mouth, feel the hot liquid going down your throat. Feel how the cup goes from a very hot temperature to a lovely warm and then to room temperature. As different thoughts enter your mind, gently return to the cup. What do you notice?

Try this living fully present exercise when playing a game with your child. Enter into the imagination: the form the Lego blocks take or how the puzzle pieces feel in your hand and fit together. Become focused on your child. As other thoughts pop into your mind (and they will) simply return to the play.

Humans learn through play and fun, so have fun. Let the child set the pace of the play, let him or her change from toy to toy and add new characters or storylines. I am often amazed at how my daughter blends toys from different sets or characters. Don't worry about packing up as you go, just for this time focus on play. Ask your child questions along the way. 'What is the name of the horse?' 'Where does this one live?' Make up stories, asking your child what happens next. Encourage and affirm all efforts. 'You are trying really hard with this puzzle.'

When children ask questions, encourage them to find their own answers. We often jump in too quickly as adults to fix things. If your child asks, 'Why do horses have tails?' or 'Why don't rainbows last very long?' respond by asking, 'Why do you think?' The responses will surprise and delight you. Encourage the 'why' questions as much as you can. Rather than feeling frustrated at the seemingly endless list of why questions that come, try to appreciate that your child is inquisitive and wants to make sense of his or her world. Children are fully engaged, trying to be fully cognizant about the world around them.

Sometimes you will be asked questions that you can't answer. Isabella recently asked me what octopi eat, and do you know, I have no idea! So we sat down at the Internet and discovered together that they eat prawns, lobsters, snails and crabs.

See each activity as an opportunity to learn and grow together. Even the most ordinary moments can show you glimpses of the extraordinary. Recently, we were visiting the Royal Botanical Gardens in Melbourne. It was a beautiful Saturday and everyone else seemed to have the same idea. We spent a long time finding a place to park and were busy getting our picnic things out of the car when Isabella asked me, 'What would happen if a rhino had no body?'

Rather than feel exasperated at the question, I replied, 'You know, I have never ever thought that, Isabella. You ask me questions that I have never ever thought of before. What do you think would happen if a rhino had no body?'

She replied, 'They wouldn't be able to run.' And she then turned around and ran off down the path laughing. I could have brushed the moment aside in my rush to unpack the car, but I am glad I didn't because now I hold that little moment dearly.

When we regularly practice living in the moment, we come to realize the joy that gets lost when we are so busy. Think about activities that you really enjoy—playing or listening to music, going for a walk, doing a craft project, gardening, having a bath. Think about how you feel when are deeply engaged in those activities; reflect on how they make you feel. It is as if time falls away and there is only you and the activity. Things seem to simplify and perspective returns. What might our lives be like if we were to live fully in the present moment? Impossible, you may say. I say, difficult, but not impossible, if we could at least allow ourselves some time during our week—an hour, a morning, a day—when we try to live fully aware and fully present! This isn't a new thing; Buddhists call it *mindfulness*. For more information you might like to read *Buddhism for Mothers* by Sarah Napthali.

Reflections for Parents

It can often be difficult for parents to find five or ten minutes of peace in a day, but the benefits of this can be significant. Maybe you could do this exercise when your child is asleep, or while your partner does the bath or even after he or she has gone to bed. You may be able to wake ten minutes earlier and grab the time then.

Go to a place where you can be quiet for five (or more) minutes. Maybe you are travelling on a train, bus or plane. Wherever you are—*wherever you are*—is a place of presence.

- Make it simple. Today you do not need candles, incense, music or a prayer shawl. No fountain, icon, chair or prayer beads. Just you and however you can show up right now, in this moment. The cosmos is big enough for all your joy and all your pain. Just show up.

- Breathe. Simply breathe. Notice the texture and temperature of the air you inhale. Breathe enough oxygen to feel movement in your body. Expand your chest and stomach.

- Exhale. Let go. Let go of everything that does not serve you or the integrity of the other. The universe knows what to do with the *let-gos*. We don't have to do anything except let go.

- Breathe in. Breathe out. Breathe in. Breathe out. Allow each inhale to be deeper, every exhale deliberate. Feel energised; move and shift in your body as your cells oxygenate.

- Awaken your senses. Be present to yourself and your surroundings. Notice what attracts your attention and stay with that. Simultaneously turn your attention to your breathing. Continue for as long as you desire. What do you notice?

- Draw in the deepest breath of your day. Perhaps the deepest breath of your life. Breathe gratitude. As you exhale, let go into the present moment.

Allow your breathing to companion you through your day. Whenever you experience stress, worry or a desire to be present more completely to a person, place, idea or the Holy One, take a five-minute break.

One of the hardest parts about silence and contemplation is having your mind wander, so here a few things that might help:

- Understand that your mind will wander; thoughts will pop into it. Just accept that it will happen

- Richard Rohr's book *Simplicity* suggests that you imagine looking out upon a fast-moving stream; every time a thought pops into your head, simply place it in a boat and send it down the river, in the boat, down the river.

- Another way is to imagine a wide blue sky and your thoughts as clouds upon the sky; let the clouds and thoughts drift away.

- Be patient with yourself.

Meditations

Breathing Technique—Mindfulness of Breath

Find a comfortable position, relax and just breathe.
Close your eyes. Big breath in.
Breathing out
Breathing in
Breathing out
Breathing in
Breathing out
Breathing in
Breathing out

Feel how the air moves into your mouth and nose, down your throat, expands into your lungs. Don't try and change your breathing, just relax.

(a few moments of silence)

When you are ready open your eyes.

After the meditation, you might like to ask your child what happened for him or her in the silence, what thoughts or images or feelings arose. If a particular image arose, you might like to ask your child to draw it. If you choose to do this meditation regularly, you can slowly extend the time of silence at the end; you might begin with ten to twenty seconds and generally extend the time to several minutes. This meditation, which focuses on the breath, is one of the most common forms of meditation. You may like to ask your child to count breaths if he or she is able; say up to ten and then back to one.

Encourage children to use this exercise if they ever find themselves scared. Just ask them to breathe deeply, right down to their tummies. Most of us only breathe using the top third or quarter of our lungs; however, we can tap into energy reserves by breathing deeply. Ask your child to place both hands over the stomach to feel the rise and fall of the tummy.

Guided Forest Meditation

Find a comfortable position.
Close your eyes. Big breath in.
Breathing in
Breathing out
Breathing in
Breathing out
Breathing in
Breathing out
Breathing in
Breathing out

Imagine you are walking in a beautiful rainforest.
It is a beautiful, warm, sunny day with a slight breeze.
All around you are tall trees soaring up into the sky.
You take your shoes and socks off and feel the soft leaves on your toes.
You notice there are some beautiful ferns around you.
You might like to pick a leaf off a tree or a flower and feel and smell it.
You can smell the fresh smell of the forest, leaves, trees and flowers.
You can feel the breeze on your face.
You can hear birds chirping in the trees.

You might be eating a yummy ice cream; taste its coolness and sweetness.
Look up into the trees. Do you see birds or little possums or maybe even some tree frogs?
It is lovely and peaceful.
You find a tall tree and sit down resting your back against the trunk.
You feel the leaves all around you.

(a few moments of silence)

Breathing

Breathe in. Breathe out. Breathe in.

Sharing the Experience

What did you see?
What did you hear?
What did you smell?
What did you taste?
What did you feel?
Try drawing the experience.

Summary

- To live fully in the moment is a gift that we can encourage in both our children and ourselves.
- See each activity as an opportunity to learn and grow together.
- Even the most ordinary moments can show you glimpses of the extraordinary.
- Rather than feeling frustrated at the seeming endless list of *why* questions that come, try to appreciate that your child is inquisitive and wants to make sense of his or her world.
- When we regularly practice living in the moment, we come to realize the joy that gets lost when we are so busy.
- Make it simple. Today you do not need candles, incense, music or a prayer shawl. No fountain, icon, chair or prayer beads. Just you and however you can show up right now, in this moment. The cosmos is big enough for all your joy and all your pain. Just show up.

Chapter 4
The Creative Heart

We are creative beings. We have two sides to our brains, the left and the right. The left part of the brain uses logic and is very detailed-oriented. It deals in words and language and tries to make sense of patterns and form strategies. It deals in the detail of life. The right side of the brain uses feelings and intuition; it is very 'big picture' focused. This is the side that engages in philosophy, religion and meaning. It likes to present possibilities and imagine what might be. It appreciates, feels gratitude and believes.

Our Western culture is very left-brain focussed. Our education system is based on the left side; we are encouraged to see the world in terms of problems that arise and methods with which to solve them. We seem to ignore that whole side of ourselves that wants to feel and intuit the way forward. Yet, as in most things, if we are able to embrace both sides, we can work towards health and wholeness.

As parents we are constantly challenged; we need to discern when a problem needs a left-brain fix—'I've lost my shoe, I saw it in the bathroom,' or when our children are upset and we know they need a cuddle and a kiss—very right brain.

When I speak of the creative heart, I mean developing and growing both sides of the brain. We are being creative when we think about how to solve a particular issue, how to decorate a room or what to have for dinner. We create our lives, our experiences. Yet we often see creativity as only relating to art or music or poetry. Our children often show us with the many pictures and drawings that arrive home from preschool that being creative is part of the normal day.

Most of us started out like this, painting and drawing, making collages and sculptures in our early childhood; and then for various reasons most of us stopped doing this. Perhaps we were told that we'd never make a living painting so it was a waste of time, or that academic schoolwork was more important. Whatever the reason, most of us rarely sit down and paint or draw a picture for fun.

We may find, though, that with children comes a return to some of these activities—colouring in, sculpting with clay or plasticine. I discovered just how much I enjoyed colouring in when Isabella began to do it. We would start doing it together but she would become interested in something else and wander off, while I would continue trying different colours, different mediums. I found it so lovely to sit and colour, to transform a black and white picture into a riot of colour. I did find, though, that I had to let go of my need for the colours to be 'right.' I would want to jump in and give Isabella a blue pencil for the sky and a yellow pencil for the sun, whereas if I let the colour choice up to her it was far more imaginative and creative than mine.

Creativity doesn't need to involve art supplies, though. Recently my daughter and I started a game just before bed. It was a silly association game. It began with her saying things such as 'what if we had a car made of popcorn?' and then I made up 'what if our house was made up of bubbles?' This went on for some time and it was a lovely creative activity.

How do we as parents and carers model creativity? This is can be a real challenge in our busy lives. Do your children ever see you enjoying creative pursuits? Not many of us knit or sew these days, but maybe we like to garden or scrapbook or bake cakes or play musical instruments. Are there any activities that you enjoyed doing before your children were born that you would like to start again? If children see their parents taking the time to be creative and have fun, they will learn the value of this.

What activities and resources might help? Young children love to make things, so it is a good idea to have materials on hand that you can change around from time to time. Here are some inexpensive and fun ideas to try:

- Play dough is always a winner. Try making your own (the recipe is in the appendix); it's easy and tends to last longer than the store bought variety.
- Paper, paint, pencils and crayons are cheap and easy to use. You can buy cheap smocks and drop sheets if you are worried about mess, or set up outside.
- You can set your children up with a box filled with stickers, pipe cleaners, glitter, pieces of felt and cardboard together with paste. This keeps them entertained and creative for ages.
- Think about natural products, too: a bucket filled with gum nuts or other seeds, different types of leaves that can be pasted onto cards or sticks collected to make models of houses or tents.
- Cheap disposable cameras are a fun way to introduce photography to children. Photos can be printed and made into 'A day in the life of...' albums. These are lovely mementos that children will enjoy looking back on.

- A shallow dish or box filled with sand can be creative. Use a fork, a spoon c fingers to make interesting patterns.
- A trough of water and food colouring can make a fun experiment.
- What about sitting down together and writing a story? Let your child choose a main character, a place to live and a story line. You can staple the pages together and ask the child to draw accompanying pictures.
- Baking cookies and biscuits using cookie cutters can amuse children for long periods of time.
- Grab a number of pots and pans and a wooden spoon and make an orchestra.

Remember, creativity doesn't just mean artistic pursuits; it can be the way in which we approach life and the opportunities that arise. Finding creative solutions can be done together with your child. Often as parents we are faced with dilemmas presented to us by others: siblings wanting to play with the same toy, or more mundane things such as no more room in the bin or a light globe popping. When you have a moment, use these opportunities to ask your child/children how they might solve the problem.

To embrace your right brain side you might like to do some art journaling. It is very easy; just pick up some pencils, crayons or pastels and have a play.

Step 1 – Try to find thirty minutes of quiet where you ideally won't be interrupted. Sit quietly and relax as much as you can. Become aware of the present moment and focus your gaze.

Step 2 – Now think about your life as it is today in this moment. There will be shades of light and dark, shapes and forms. Spend a few moments just thinking about the elements that make up your life. When you are ready ask yourself, 'What is my life like today?' Focus on this question. Try to just be, appreciating your role in your life.

Step 3 – Now pick up the pencils or crayons and respond to the question by drawing. Try not to over-think the process, just choose colours and represent your life on the paper.

Step 4 – When you come to a natural end, place the drawing in front of you and spend some time looking at your picture. Try not to judge yourself, just gaze. Look for lines, shapes, colours and forms. You might ask yourself why some colours are larger than olhers. You may be able to see the relationships between colours or shapes. What is the level of energy or intensity like? Are there colours or shapes that overlap each other?

Step 5– In each stage of our lives we are being offered an invitation—perhaps an invitation for growth, for change or for healing. Is there an invitation here for you today?

Step 6 – You mighl like to give your drawing a title. Jot it on the back with the date.

Reflection for Children

Try a similar exercise with your child based upon one of the meditations. After you have finished one of the meditations from this book or one you have written, provide your child with some pencils or crayons and ask him or her to draw what he or she might have seen during the meditation.

Meditations

The Prayer of Quiet/Contemplation

Find a comfortable position.
Focus in your breathing.
Imagine it moving in ... and out of your body
In ... and out ... in ... and out.
Let the breath carry you deeper into a quiet place.
Don't force anything ... just let the breath carry you ... deeper ...
and deeper.
Just breathe in and out, in and out.
Let your breathing carry you deeper ... into a quiet place.

You are being invited into a special room. As you enter the room,
you see that it is an art studio. Around the room are paintbrushes,
clay for sculpture, cameras to take photos, pens for writing,
musical instruments to play, wool and paper for craft and beautiful
food to cook with.

Take some time just to be in this room: touch each thing, imagine
how you might use it, but you don't need to choose anything right
now. Just be in this room. There is only love and affirmation in
this room.

When you are ready, choose an activity. There is no need to hurry.

(pause)

Now have fun, play with your creativity. Imagine what you can
do. Imagine the beauty that you are able to create. If you hear any
negative thoughts, simply return to the creativity.

(long pause)

When you think you have finished, just be with your newly
creative object of beauty. Hold it gently.

(pause)

When you are ready, gradually and gently bring yourself to the
present time and place. Take all the time you need to make the
transition.

Painting with Colour Meditation

Find a comfortable position and close your eyes.
Take a big breath in, big breath out.

Imagine you are in a big, safe room filled with paints of every colour. You see a large blank picture next to you. When you are ready, pick up a paintbrush.
Choose a colour and paint on the blank picture. Choose as many colours as you would like. Make the painting as big or as small as you like; paint whatever topic you would like to. If you make a mistake, just clear it in your mind.

Take as long as you like. You can always come back to this room and paint whenever you would like to.

(pause for a few minutes)

When you are ready open your eyes.

Summary

- The left part of our brain uses logic and is very detailed-oriented. It deals in words and language and tries to make sense of patterns and form strategies. It deals in the detail of life.
- The right side of our brain uses feelings and intuition and is very 'big picture' focused. This is the side that engages in philosophy, religion and meaning. It likes to present possibilities and imagine what might be. It appreciates, feels gratitude and believes.
- When we speak of a creative heart, we are looking to develop and grow both sides of our brains.
- If children see their parents taking the time to be creative and have fun, they will learn the value of this.

Chapter 5
The Natural Heart

What do I mean by a natural heart? I am thinking about children who have the opportunity to spend time playing outside, finding little bugs and creatures, collecting sticks and rocks, and getting their hands dirty. Children who are able to see the seasons change and clouds move across the sky, who can feel the rain on their hands and faces.

As parents we have become very protective of our children. We like to supervise them when they are outside ,and this is completely appropriate sometimes. But it would be nice to think that children could have some time playing with their siblings or friends on their own, allowing them to jump and climb and run without supervision. When I think back to my childhood, the times I enjoyed the most involved making mud pies or riding my bike around the block, walking to the park with a friend and spending lazy afternoons swinging on the swings.

A simple activity such as growing some tomato plants or herbs in a window box are amazing opportunities for children to learn about the natural environment, seeds, dirt, water, sun and even death when plants may not flourish; also the seasons, cooking and taste.

Part of the learning philosophy of the preschools and infant/toddler centres of Reggio Emilia is the concept that the environment is the third teacher alongside teachers and parents. Children learn from both the indoor and outdoor environments. Inside the home, children learn about relationships and family dynamics, as well as mediums such as pencils, paper, glue and glitter. Outdoors, children learn how the natural world works, about seasons, about water and about animals and insects. If children are raised separated from the natural environment, they lose their place in the world.

'If we want children to flourish, to become truly empowered, then let us allow them to love the earth before we ask them to save it.' David Sobel, *Beyond Eco.*

Never before has there been such an urgency to protect our natural environment. We have come to realize that the way in which we have used the environment for our own needs and wants has come at a very high cost. We now have a wonderful opportunity to model a more sustainable way of living to our children.

Water – No other element in nature sustains us as water does; human bodies are made up of around 65 percent water. We use water for so many of our daily activities: washing, eating, cooking, playing and bathing. At my daughter's school there are water tanks installed and children are encouraged to play with water, but only while there is water in the tanks. When tanks are dry, it provides an opportunity to discuss why there is no water. In drought-stricken Melbourne, we have been forced to introduce tough water restrictions on watering our gardens and washing cars due to severe drops in our water catchment dams. We have had below average rainfall for over a decade now, so much so that rain and even garden sprinklers have become a novelty. What a shame that Isabella hasn't felt the sheer thrill of playing under a sprinkler or filling up a little wading pool and lolling around on a summer afternoon. I need to explain to her that we can only use the backyard taps a couple of times a week.

We can, however, model water conservation by collecting water at the tap into a bucket to later put on the garden, by collecting water from the first few seconds of the shower before the water warms up and by collecting bath water. This leads to a wide range of conversations from soaps and chemicals to hoses, pipes, gravity and the rain cycle. If you have the chance to install a water tank in your home, this is a great way to show how water is collected. Even water collected in buckets during a shower can lead to chats about measurements and numbers.

Waste – A recent study shows that Australian families throw away about one fifth of the food they buy. How do we model to our children a better way? Most families now have recycling bins, which offer an opportunity to show our children what we can recycle. As you dispose of something, begin to ask your child if it is something that can go in the recycle bin. If it can, great. If not, why not? This can be a great opportunity to discuss waste with your child. Think about exploring the following questions with your child:

- Where does rubbish go once it leaves the house?
- Where does the rubbish truck take the rubbish?
- Do we need to clean bottles and containers before we recycle them?
- How could we reduce the amount of rubbish we have?

About a third of the rubbish in bins is food material. You might like to consider a compost bin for unused fruit and vegetable scraps, or a worm farm. We bought a worm farm for the house and it has been great fun. We collect up the worm castings and choose the plants that will receive them. Isabella and I also take out our collected food scraps and give them to the worms.

There are a myriad of ways we can reduce waste, including reducing the amount of packaging and plastic bags we use. You might like to give your child a reusable bag to take shopping with you. You probably have clothes or toys that your child has grown out of. This is a good opportunity to look at the best way to recycle these items. Could you have a garage sale at your house or donate the goods to a charity?

Transport – This is where families living in the inner cities have such an advantage over their country and suburban friends. Thinking about, discussing and debating how we get around both in our daily lives and on holidays will spark off interest and consideration in our children. If it is possible to walk or take a bike, then try it as often as you are able. When you are purchasing a new car, include your children in the discussion about fuel economy and petrol use. Think also about how far our food has travelled to get to our home. My daughter loves strawberries and blueberries, and whenever we go to the supermarket she asks for them. Signage has improved greatly, so it is now possible to see where our food was grown. This can lead to some interesting debates about whether it is good to be eating fruit in the off-season when it has travelled so far. I still think a snack of strawberries even in the off-season it better than biscuits, so we can only try our best.

This isn't meant to instil guilty feelings and make every buying decision agony, just simply to promote awareness and opportunities for discussion with our children.

Biodiversity – This is an interesting concept. It is simply the idea that we make it possible for the most plants and animals to exist in our world. At a global level it can incorporate the extinction and endangerment of plants and animals, while at a local level it can be about the sorts of plants and trees we might grow in our backyard to encourage birds and butterflies to live there. Or it might mean growing a wide variety of herbs and vegetables in our vegetable patches.

Energy – When I was in primary school we had a visit from a group who performed a show all about 'ergs.' Ergs are cute little critters made up of energy. Every appliance and machine produced ergs, and we were shown how ergs could escape. For example, if a window was left open and the heater was on, then ergs from the heater could escape and be wasted. It was such a simple concept that it has stayed with me. I always look to see if ergs can escape. A simple idea like this can help children become aware of how we use energy in the home. An energy meter can also be used to show how energy consumption increases when different appliances are turned on.

Reflection for Parents

Thinking back on your childhood, respond to the following questions:

- What activities did you enjoy the most?

- How do we live in a way that is more sympathetic to the natural environment?

- How do we as parents and carers model living naturally?

- What activities and resources might help us?

Useful Meditations

So far in this book, we have looked at meditations that involve relaxing and closing our eyes, but there are other forms of meditation. One way to meditate is to undertake a walking meditation. This involves simply walking in your local neighbourhood in a mindful way. As you walk, notice the sounds, the birds, the local children, a stereo, someone practicing a musical instrument, a car starting, a passing motorbike. Notice the trees, the plants, the flowers, the gardens. What do you smell? Can you smell a distinctive flower or leaf, someone's cooking? What does it feel like to walk across the footpath or grass? Can you feel the sun on you? Are there any clouds in the sky?

This is a lovely exercise to do with your child. Encourage him or her to be as quiet as possible, and ask what he or she can see, smell, feel or hear.

Below are some other activities you can do with your child to touch the spirituality of nature:

- Lying on the ground, watch clouds and see if you can make shapes out of them.

- At a local park, see if you can collect a single leaf from each plant or tree.
- At a local park, see how many sticks or pebbles/stones you can collect.
- If you are able to get to a beach, take your shoes off and feel the sand and lapping waves on your feet and hands. Collect shells and see if you can see any fish or other creatures in the water. Watch the waves.
- Make a daisy chain.
- Make mud pies.
- Collect flowers.
- Search for a four-leaf clover.
- Plant some vegetables, herbs or seedlings.
- Have a picnic in your backyard.
- Spend some time barefoot.

Guided Meditations

Beach Meditation

Breathing

Find a comfortable position.
Close your eyes.
Big breath in.
Breathing out
Breathing in
Breathing out
Breathing in
Breathing out
Breathing in
Breathing out

Imagine you are walking along a beach. It is a beautiful, warm, sunny day with a slight breeze. The waves are gently lapping on the sand. You take your shoes and socks off and feel the sand in between your toes. You notice there are some beautiful shells lying on the beach. Pick one up if you would like. You can smell the salty water. You can feel the breeze on your face. You might be eating a yummy ice cream. Taste its coolness and sweetness. You can hear the seagulls flying above you.

Look out to sea. Do you see people swimming or maybe some boats? It is lovely and peaceful. You find a spot and sit down. Feel the sand around you. Look out at the waves. Waves coming in and going out. Waves coming in and going out. Waves coming in and going out. Waves coming in and going out.

(a few moments of silence)

Breathing
Breathe in. Breathe out. Breathe in

Sharing the Experience

What did you see?
What did you hear?
What did you smell?
What did you taste?
What did you feel?

Summary

- Children with a natural heart have the opportunity to spend time playing outside, finding little bugs and creatures, collecting sticks and rocks and getting their hands dirty.
- Children with a natural heart are able to see the seasons change and clouds move across the sky, and feel the rain on their hands and face.
- Never before has there been such an urgency to protect our natural environment. We now have a wonderful opportunity to model a more sustainable way of living to our children.
- There are five main areas which we can explore for a more sustainable way of life:
  o Water
  o Waste
  o Biodiversity
  o Transport
  o Energy

Chapter 6
The Reflective Heart

To be reflective means that we allow time both as adults and children to think back over events in our lives in order to glean further understanding. This reflection can be a simple activity such as what we enjoyed most and least about our day, or a longer process in which we might keep a journal or speak with a counsellor or Spiritual Director regularly. The pace of today's life means that this process can be forgotten or rushed through; other things crowd in, to-do lists stare at us.

Socrates said that 'an unexamined life is not worth living.' If that is true, how do we examine our lives and at what age is it appropriate to begin? I think the word *examine* brings with it a clinical or formal approach. What I would like to invite you to do instead is just think back over the past twenty-four hours or so; think about the moments you enjoyed and why you enjoyed them. What did it feel like at the time? When did those feelings change? What about times you found difficult—why were they difficult? What feelings arose in you? Think about conversations you may have had. Did they flow easily or were they challenging? Were there things you said that you regret? Or things you wish you had said? Be gentle on yourself here; this isn't meant to be an opportunity to chastise yourself, simply to acknowledge an observation and move on.

Children's lives offer a myriad of opportunities for reflection: playing with friends, times when they became upset, things they thought were funny or amusing. Sometimes children will become upset and we can't always see the reason. I find it useful at a later stage in their development to ask them to reflect on what made them upset. They may not know, but sometimes they are able to articulate what they were feeling at the time.

It can be tempting as parents to gloss over things or offer advice. We need to learn that children often don't want advice, just understanding. For example, they may say that a friend was mean to them. As parents we want to avoid pain and discomfort in our children, so we may want to jump in and tell them not to play with that particular friend. However, there is an opportunity here to value our children's feelings and respect them. Simply acknowledge that it is not nice when friends are mean and that it can make us sad. The child will feel heard and validated. Obviously if the child is in danger of being physically or emotionally hurt, then we must take steps to avoid this. However, if the conflict is a matter of normal relationships and friendships, then we can empower our children to solve things for themselves.

You may be wondering what good can come of rehashing events that have already happened. This is a good question, because doing this seems to run counter to encouraging us to live in the moment and be fully present. However, for our sense of wellbeing we need both. In reflecting on a particular difficultly we may start to see a pattern. We may glimpse an understanding that we did not see at the time. We may appreciate a moment of clarity or beauty that we missed.

How We Learn

As adults we all learn and take in information differently. There are three main ways of processing information. Most of us have a preference but we will use all three in the course of our day.

- Visual

- Auditory
- Kinaesthetic

Visual

A person with a visual preference tends to like to see information displayed in some form to make sense of it. These people love drawings, sketches, diagrams, maps and pictures. They need to 'see' the map to make sense of where they are going. Interestingly, they often use visual words in their speech, for example:

- We'll see about that.
- I need to look for a solution.
- Picture this!
- I can see you don't understand.

Auditory

People who have an auditory preference like to hear and read things to process information. They prefer reading instructions before setting out. They think in words and respond well in lectures and talks. They like to write to-do lists and make notes. Their language also reflects their learning preference:

- I hear what you are saying.
- I can read him/her like a book.

- Can you summarise what you just said?

Kinaesthetic

A person with a kinaesthetic preference likes to carry out a physical activity rather than watching a demonstration or listening to the explanation. This person learns through doing, experiencing, touching, moving and being. He or she often has a good sense of balance, timing and rhythm, and is good at sports. These people use words such as these:

- Can I have a go at that?
- Let's try to finish this.
- Work with me on this.
- I have a gut feeling about this.

When it comes to our children it can be tempting to begin to define their learning preference, but try to avoid this. Instead provide the widest possible set of experiences for them to try new things, eat new foods, meet new people and see new places.

The Reggio Emilia philosophy looks at the one hundred languages of the child.

The child

is made of one hundred.
The child has
a hundred languages
a hundred hands
a hundred thoughts
a hundred ways of thinking
of playing, of speaking.
A hundred always a hundred
ways of listening
of marvelling of loving
a hundred joys
for singing and understanding
a hundred worlds
to discover
a hundred worlds
to invent
a hundred worlds
to dream.
The child has
a hundred languages

(and a hundred hundred hundred more)
but they steal ninety-nine.
The school and the culture
separate the head from the body.
They tell the child:
to think without hands
to do without head
to listen and not to speak
to understand without joy
to love and to marvel
only at Easter and at Christmas.
They tell the child:
to discover the world already there
and of the hundred
they steal ninety-nine.
They tell the child:
that work and play
reality and fantasy
science and imagination
sky and earth
reason and dream

are things
that do not belong together.
And thus they tell the child
that the hundred is not there.
The child says:
No way. The hundred is there.

Loris Malaguzzi
(translated by Lella Gandini)

Reflection for Parents

Life Map

Take a large piece of paper and some pencils. Draw a line representing you~
out roughly every five or ten years of primary school, secondary school and post schoo.
studies, giving yourself lots of space. Now begin by placing in key events in your life.
These may be things such as the birth of siblings, starting school, moving house, deaths
of significant people and moments of success or failure. There is no right or wrong, just
write them down when they pop into your head. Even small events can be significant.
You may like to have a break and return to it later or a number of times.

When you have completed it, take some time just looking at the life map. Are there any
periods of your life that seemed to be busier than others? Were there periods of your life
when little seemed to occur? Are there any patterns that may be forming?

Life's Stepping-stones

One interesting question to ask ourselves is 'what are the key moments or events that
have bought me to this present moment?'

This exercise is very different to the previous exercise. You may find events arise that
were key turning points or moments of clarity or decision.

s exercise invites you to enter a place of quiet and stillness. As you reflect on your life there may be images that arise—events, feelings, situations. Don't judge them, just sit with them and note them down. Don't worry about the chronological order in which they appear. Come up with eight to twelve key events. When you feel that you have come to the end, record and number the stepping-stones. You may want to give each a title or short phrase. Now take a moment to reread each moment; you may find it helpful to read these out loud.

As you read each point slowly, enter into the experience of each stepping-stone. You may like to record any thoughts or feelings that have stirred in you during the reading.

Now look back over the two exercises. You will find they both have very different qualities.

Our Sacred Stories

What are the stories that have shaped our lives? If we were to speak with someone we had never met before, how would we tell our stories? Where would we begin? What would we share and not share? Our stories are sacred and unique.

For children the use of stories and fairy tales is a beautiful way to begin to explore this. I am often surprised that my daughter chooses the same story before bed for weeks on end. What does she like about this particular story? What engages her? What sparks her imagination? What characters does she like to and relate to? What words does she like to hear?

These can be great questions to ask our children. Children often reflect back and incorporate stories into their lives. For an exercise such as reflecting on the day it can often be an event in a book that they most enjoyed. Maybe at an early age they don't see books as outside of themselves. Perhaps the stories become part of them.

If you are able, jot down some of the funny stories from your child's early years. Children will arrive at a point when they absolutely love hearing stories of when they threw up on you or your partner or when they poured their pureed apples on top of their heads.

Reflection for Younger Children

Choose a story and read it to your child. It doesn't matter which book. After reading the story ask your child the following questions:

- Did you like the story? Why?
- Which character did you like the best? The least?
- What was your favourite part?
- What would you do if you were that character?

- How would you feel if you were that character?

Reflection for Older Children

Once children are able to read and write, encourage them to keep a journal. Make sure they feel safe in writing in the journal and let them know that it is theirs and no one else will read it. Allow your child to choose a journal or decorate one as it pleases him or her.

Meditations

We are going to have a time of reflection.

Begin by finding a comfortable position and closing your eyes.

Become aware of what is happening within you at this moment.
Gently bring your attention to your body.
How are you feeling?
Notice any parts of your body that are tense.
Allow them to relax.

Now become aware of how you're feeling.
Notice any anger, any sadness.
Simply note where you feel them without trying to change them.
Notice any happiness or peace
Just let them be.
Now bring attention to your breath.
Breathe in and breathe out.
Just notice your breath without trying to change it.
Breathe in and breathe out.
In and out.

You will become aware of a great peacefulness and silence upon you.

Feel how good it is to be here now.
To just be.

(a period of silence)

When you are ready come back to the room.

Slowly move your body.

Open your eyes.

Meditations

We are going to have a time of reflection.

Begin by finding a comfortable position and closing your eyes.

Become aware of what is happening within you at this moment.
Gently bring your attention to your body.
How are you feeling?
Notice any parts of your body that are tense.
Allow them to relax.

Now become aware of how you're feeling.
Notice any anger, any sadness.
Simply note where you feel them without trying to change them.
Notice any happiness or peace
Just let them be.
Now bring attention to your breath.
Breathe in and breathe out.
Just notice your breath without trying to change it.
Breathe in and breathe out.
In and out.

You will become aware of a great peacefulness and silence upon you.

Feel how good it is to be here now.
To just be.

(a period of silence)

When you are ready come back to the room.

Slowly move your body.

Open your eyes.

Summary

- To be reflective means that we allow time both as adults and children to think back over events in our lives to glean further understanding.
- The pace of today's life means that this process can be forgotten or rushed through.
- Children's lives offer a myriad of opportunities for reflection: playing with friends, times when they became upset, things they thought were funny or amusing.

Conclusion

The most beautiful gift we can give our children is time and space. Time to explore the world around them, time to learn about themselves, time to learn what is means to be and the space to do that in.

Appendix

Recipe for play dough

Ingredients:

2 cups plain flour
4 tablespoons cream of tartar
2 tablespoons cooking oil
1 cup of salt
Food colouring
2 cups of water

Method

Mix the ingredients in a saucepan, stir over medium heat for 3-5 minutes or until mixtures thickens.

Writing Your Meditations

I really encourage you to write your own meditations. You may choose your child's favourite place, a garden, the zoo, a playground, a grandparent's house, a favourite holiday spot. There is no right or wrong way; by simply being preset to your child, your voice and your presence will be a special gift for him or her. You will note that I have followed a similar plan for both of my guided meditations:

- Begin with breathing.

- Introduce the location.

- Engage the five senses. Have a little fun here, play around with smells, shapes, colours or just keep things simple and let your children fill in the gaps.

- Spend some time of quiet.

- Return to breathing.

- Ask questions. I find asking questions around the five senses works well:
    o What did you see?
    o What did you hear?

o   What did you feel?
o   What did you smell?
o   What did you taste?

Further Reading

Napthali, Sarah, *Buddhism for Mothers*. Allen & Unwin, NSW Australia 2003.

Tolle, Eckhart, *The Power of Now*. Hodder Mobius, London 1999.

Linn, Dennis, Sheila Fabricant, Matthew, *Sleeping with Bread: Holding What Gives You Life*. Paulist Press, NJ 1994.

Boyd Cadwell, Lucy, *Bringing Reggio Emilia Home*. Teachers College Press, New York 1997.